DISTRIBUTE RIGHT

SURE SHOT WAY TO MAKE YOUR DISTRIBUTION BUSINESS A WEALTH MAKING MACHINE

DISTRIBUTE RIGHT

SURE SHOT WAY TO MAKE YOUR DISTRIBUTION BUSINESS A WEALTH MAKING MACHINE

By

SACHIN AGARWAL

Worldwide Publishing by
Pendown Press

PENDOWN PRESS

An ISO 9001 & ISO 14001 Certi ied Co.,
Regd. O ice: 2525/193, 1st Floor, Onkar Nagar-A,
Tri Nagar, Delhi-110035
Ph.: 09350849407, 09312235086
E-mail: info@pendownpress.com
Branch O ice: 1A/2A, 20, Hari Sadan, Ansari Road,
Daryaganj, New Delhi-110002
Ph.: 011-45794768
Website: PendownPress.com

First Edition: 2021

ISBN: 978-93-90479-20-7

Layout and Cover Designed by Pendown Graphics Team

Printed and Bound in India by Thomson Press India Ltd.

CONTENTS

THE SACHIN STORY

I was a distributor of a renowned brand in 2013, and I was very passionate about that brand, also I was passionate to grow. I thought company would bring big opportunity for me.

In 2014, I was attending one of the reward conference of the company and I stood number 3 in india… while coming back from stage,

Can u imagine what was the question in the back of my mind, I want to become number 1.

And next year I DID IT. then my mama, who is also a partner in my business called me and congratulated me, but asked sarcastically about the profits and the debtors list and the non moving stocks…

This sarcasm moved me, I respect my mama a lot, because he has taught me a lot. And I saw that my profits were low, my debtors list soared and there were some good non-moving stocks.

ALTHOUGH I WAS NUMBER ONE IN INDIA. Distributors sometimes forget that in a business is he adding any value ? If not to increase in sales by diminishing margin remains the only way, which may be completely a bad strategy.

Now either you add value in the business, or decrease margins... generally people choose the second path along with that give credits beyond limits, which may prove dangerous to any business. We need to be careful about our decision and understand that we work for profits.

CHAPTER-1

THE REAL CAUSE OF LIFESTYLE DISORDERS

Who am I?

I am Sachin Agarwal. I have been into battery and UPS business for around 20 years from now, with my brother Sumit Agarwal.

We started with a battery spares shop. Our uncle Mr. Deepak Mittal (whom we respect a lot) introduced us to this business in the year 2000, one day's turnover then was rs. 10,000.

We took distribution of several top inverter-batteries brand gradually. We had a passion to grow. We worked really hard. We opened 5 outlets in Bangalore and built a presence in South India.

Our biggest observation were

1. The brands were growing but the distributors were not.

2. The brands used the platform of the distributor and forget them when the brand grew.

3. The distributors' future was not secure.

Why I am writing this booklet?

1. To create awareness among the distributors, how brands and channel sales work.

2. To help distributors grow their business.

3. Generate better opportunity for distributors.

In this book, you will learn

1. Mistakes that generally people commit before choosing a brand for distribution.

2. How to grow profits in distribution business.

3. Choosing entry and exit strategy to get extra mileage in distribution business.

CHAPTER-2

WHAT IS THE ROLE OF THE DISTRIBUTOR?

The distributor is the middle men between the manufacturer and the retailer, or between the manufacturer and businesses that integrate the product or use it for their own consumption. There can be a chain of distributors, for example a global distributor who sells to specialised distributors for certain industries. In B2B markets, e.g. for desks, complicated machinery or cleaning services, you generally have no retailers.

The main assets of a distributor are his sales force, transportation means and storage. He will try to optimise the margin he can get with these assets. So it helps if you create an easy ordering process for him, with packaging that he can easily split and handle, and good documentation for his sales force.

Average retail margin and distribution margin

Product category	Distributor	Retailer
Fast moving consumer goods	3-10%	8-40%
Clothing and apparel	15-30%	20-50%
Electronics like mobile phones	3-7%	3-7%
Cars		5-15%
Furniture		30-50%
Jewelry		30-60%
Electrical equipment and lights	5-7%	15-25%

Please note that these figures are indications and especially for distributors heavily depend on the tasks that a distributor should do. For fast moving consumer goods 3 to 10% may be fine for just the physical distribution, but if the distributor should also do promotional efforts, this percentage should be much higher. Therefore we have to look into detail in the various roles of the parties in the distribution chain.

CHAPTER-3

AFTER SALES SERVICE

Before I share the core content of the book, I would like to share a story.

So the story is of Ram who used to make water coolers, assemble the motors and different parts and used to sell himself to customers.

He himself gave the required after sales service to the customer, whenever required. Customers were happy with him. And all his business ran through referrals.

One day a -newly launched brand 'X' came to Ram, and said, "Why do you do so much of hard work?" We will give you packed product, and you just need to sell to your customers. We will also provide after sales service. We will also give you rewards and foreign trips on the achievement of targets.

Ram saw the flashy picture and took the distribution of the brand. Slowly Ram left his own assembling thing and started selling only branded products.

Slowly the 'X' brand got several other distributors like Ram and it got established in market. Now brand 'X' started giving targets to Ram and on non-accomplishment of targets, it said that it will find new distributor.

Now, the complete control on Ram's business was of the brand. Because, one of the reasons was also that Ram stopped serving his customers for after sales.

Brand started becoming more and more popular among his customers too. The importance which Ram had, when he had aligned with brand X, started diminishing gradually.. Because, BRAND GREW BUT RAM DID NOT. And this Ram is no one else, but it's mine and your story.

CHAPTER-4

ABOUT ME

Hello everyone, I am Sachin Agarwal. After being a distributor and struggler in business today, I have already launched a brand in lead acid battery industry in the name of REDON. And I am damn sure that this is going to become a 1,000 cr. brand.

I have been based in Bangalore since 1999. We have stood highest selling distributors for top brands in inverter battery industry for several years. In 2006 we started with Microtek, 2008 with Exide. We still distribute these brands. In 2012, we started distributing luminous and stopped in 2018. Since then, we have been doing only one thing that is building our own brand, so that we can serve maximum people. Now, we have taken so many initiatives that our target is clearly visible to us.

Recently, me and my brother Sumit Agarwal were covered by Economic Times and also in The Indian Express as a success story from scratch. Kenfolios, a digital magazine also covered our success story. Today, we have a loyal and loving team of 100 plus people which is set to grow.

Helping a business grow is the biggest charity in this world. This is the one thing I understand totally.

There are three aspects which will build our brand. As a personality—Number one is The Emotion behind the brand, because I have seen biggest struggles of business and I had no one in my life who could have held my hand and told that these are the right steps that you need to take in business. So, I am that person who wants to help others with his experience and help people grow, and I am evolving every day.

I have seen that brands do not have any concern about the growth of the distributor. Brands only use distributors to grow, blunt but truth. So, this is the logic. This is number two.

I know that people want to grow but do not have an understanding as to what to do and what not to do. And this is the facility which I am going to give to the people in business so that they can really grow.

And I am selfish, this is number three because if I help my distributors grow, my business will grow automatically…

So, with these three aspects, the Emotion, this logic, this reason, and being selfish… Brand REDON will be built.

I have understood that in my journey I have learnt a lot being a distributor and now being an owner of brand. There are several mistakes that distributors make, which stop them to grow. So, I thought to put my thoughts here, to enable people take help out of my thought and grow.

After reading this book, you will understand the power of distribution business. Why we distributors are very important for any brand's business.

CHAPTER-5

MISTAKES PEOPLE DO BEFORE STARTING A DISTRIBUTION

1. What mistakes generally people do before starting a distribution?

    a. **They don't interview the founder. Example:** A Chai franchisee closed down after opening 20 outlets and the supports were not given after that. Because the founder was not determined enough or he got some other better opportunities. One of my friends lost his money, without any mistake on his side.

    b. **They see the flashy picture and not the margins:** Sometimes, we get carried away with the designs of brand and the script of the sales managers. And do not check the basics. For example:

- Number of years company has been into this business,

- Competition analysis

- Investors' detail or financial background of the founders, etc.

c. **They don't understand what the company is looking from them. For example:** one of my friends was looking for a distribution of a newly launched laptop company. I would not mention the brand here. The manager said current investment would be 34 cr. and later on 20 cr. Now, when the friend asked me should I take this up or not, my answer was see what investment they are looking for you. Gradually, the second year you would have pressure to invest 2-3 cr. again, else parallel new distributors will be appointed. And I left this on his choice.

d. **They don't understand the journey of product** and which level of product they want to invest in and where they want to exit. There always comes a level, when a product becomes a commodity, choice should be of distributor, whether he wants to continue with low margin or diversify.

e. **They never meet existing distributors.** This is simple but silly mistake by distributors.

CHAPTER-6

HOW BRAND OPERATES

---

1. First, when a brand comes to the market, it tries to do business with people (DISTRIBUTORS) who have existing network of dealers so that they can register faster growth.

2. To get those dealers, higher margin is given to the distributors.

3. After hijacking the network, they increase the margin of dealers and decrease the same for the distributors. Now, distributors become less relevant.

4. Then brand starts advertising and hacks the customer because from now onwards, material is available with the dealers...

And now brand is created. Once it's done, brand doesn't listen to any one and talks only to customers.

My question here is: Did the distributor contribute to build the brand?

Does he have any share in the brand?

Should the distributor have any share in the brand?

Your answers are the story. Now the time has come to understand the value of our business and start asking for more.

Initial Distributors who put their hard work and invest their time, money, effort, and everything to build brand, should get more.

CHAPTER-7

HOW DISTRIBUTORS CAN INCREASE THEIR BUSINESS?

---

1. **Working with the right team**

   a. Companies do it for themselves but never teach the distributors how to hire right candidates. Hiring right candidates is a process and science, if done rightly, it can change the fate of business.

   b. If the team is not right, the burden of work comes back on the entrepreneur and he becomes one of the hardest working persons in the business, which may not be the right thing.

> c. Entrepreneurs' main work should be strategy and sales and thinking how to double the profits

2. Calculate and focus on monthly profits, because ultimately we do business to earn profits.

I have met around 2000 dealers in last 3 years. When I spoke to them one on one, and asked about calculation of profits, I found that only 2-3% of people were calculating their monthly profits. I was surprised to see that. If Sachin Tendulkar doesn't know what is his score, how would he bat or plan for a century. Similarly profit is the score board of our business.

Generally I have seen people focusing just on turnover, its my humble request to distributors to work on profitable business only and focus on profits. As its rightly said, 'what you focus on, improves'

3. Solve your customer's problems

Once I went to buy a trouser of blackberry brand. (One of my favourite brands). I tried two trousers of same style but of different sizes—one was 32 and other was 34. 32 was good fit but, was tight at tummy. 34 size was loose for me. I din't buy that time. Next time, when I went for shopping, the sales guy requested me to try 32 size again. This time the magic was that they had put a spring on the hook of trouser. This helped me to adjust that 32 size on my waist. Amazing, they solved my problem. And I'm their brand ambassador (promoting brand here).

Similarly, are you solving your customers' problems?

Else if you do not add any value in a supply chain, you will be evicted today or tomorrow or you will keep playing the game of low margins.

4. **Solve your company's problems**

    Just try to solve your customers' problems. Are you solving your company's problems too? Your relationship with the company will grow. You may get some more new opportunities, may be a bigger region to distribute their products.

5. **Build the right network, be available with the people**

    Are you meeting your dealers regularly? Are you meeting your business fraternity regularly?

6. **Diversify**

    Is there a way that you can utilize the same infrastructure, same set of customers to sell more variety of products, that can quickly add some numbers to your profits?

7. **Learn**

    The biggest challenge in our business community is that we don't learn from different resources. If we attend lots of webinars and meet mentors and hire some coaches for business, a lot can change in the business.

8. **Understand the product journey and make the entry-exit strategy**

When product comes to market

a. Risk is moderately high

b. More work for distributor to do, to create awareness

c. Obviously the brand would share more margins with the distributor, so the profits are high

d. Money rotation is a bit low

When Product gets established

a. The product becomes a brand

b. It's just like a commodity

c. Margins are reduced

d. Risk is low

e. Money rotation is faster

We need to decide carefully when to enter and when to exit, and even though we continue, how to diversify.

CHAPTER-8

THE UPCOMING CHALLENGES

---

1. Udaan

2. Big basket

3. Ship rocket

4. Of-business

5. Companies focussing on several channels

6. Your money your concern

All these companies which I have mentioned here are amazing startups, few are on establishing stage. These companies will bring big disruption in distribution industry.

Udaan is connecting the manufacturers and dealers directly. One of the subsidiaries of UDAAN is even financing the dealers, which can be a big threat to traditional distribution business.

Big-basket is eating up the grocers' business, (no offence to big basket although, they are doing their work), of-business is a non- banking financial institutions, which can finance the dealers.

All these I'm sharing just as examples of how things are changing.

I saw the Ad. of ship rocket promising to stock and deliver any product at rs. 10 per order. (Just for example)

Awareness would help us take necessary steps in case of need.

CHAPTER-9

THE GROWTH GRAPH

The growth graph of any business can be upward trending only; it cannot be flat. **Nothing in this universe is stagnant, either it is growing or it is dying.** Similarly in our business, either we are growing or we are dying the graph is never flat.

And now the most interesting part is that the growth path is never a straight line…

This every distributor needs to understand. The responsibility of growth of your business is on you. At the time, when business is running flawlessly, it's not the time to sit back. This is the time to think and grow your hunger for more.

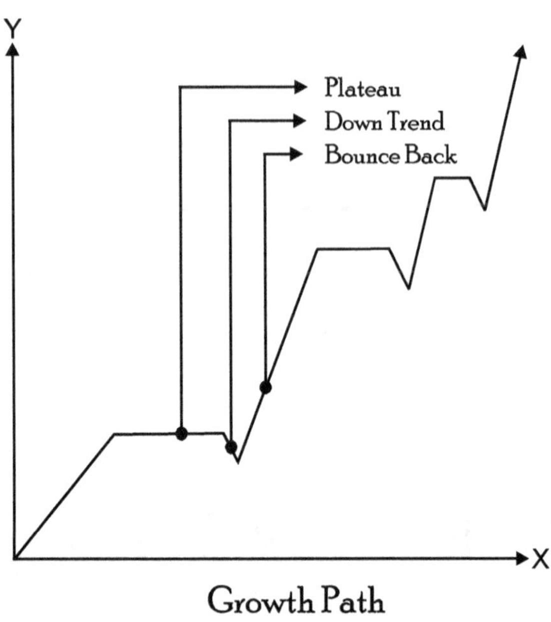

Growth Path

CHAPTER-10

HOW A BUSINESS GROWS

Now, whatever I am writing, I'm writing with my own core experience… and this chapter mat looks a bit irrelevant, but trust me, this is one of the most relevant chapters.

Businesses grow when you grow emotionally, physically, spiritually as well as mentally.

The 20:20:20 formula of Robin Sharma has made me successful. The exercises for first 20 mins. of a day has helped me improve metabolism, the meditation for 20 mins. has helped me focus more on business. The 20 mins. of planning gave me clarity on my actions.

Also, most importantly I could resonate so much from the book **extreme you, step up, standout, kick ass repeat** by Sarah robb o hagan.

I have worked out in gym a lot. When I first joined gym, my brother laughed and told me how many days will go to gym I will see. But I continued for 6 months relentlessly. And built a fair physique. Not only that, it has helped me to build lasersharp focus.

Suggestion: follow the free videos of Robin Sharma on youtube, to understand this more.

CHAPTER-11

WHY CUSTOMERS COME TO A DEALER?

---

1. The customer of a small dealer comes to him either to buy a new product:

   a. His journey starts with a place where he doesn't know his requirements

   b. The dealer understands the need and suggests the customer a particular product

   c. The dealer builds the trust, and then pitches a price

   d. Negotiation is done and a deal is closed

   e. Dealer delivers/installs a product at the customer place and collects the payment

    f. Dealer collects the feedback of the journey of the customer too

2. Next time, the customer approaches the dealer in case the product is not functioning properly or he is facing the problem.

At this phase, the biggest mistake that we commit is to push the customers to call the customer care and not address the complaint himself (may not be relevant to few products!), but if the dealer helps the customer, the customer becomes loyal to the dealer and this is something not everyone understands.

So, we need to understand this and make the dealers understand that you should be the brand and build the personal brand of your shop or your business so big that the customer should buy what you sell and not the other way round.

Elephant training

I hope you know how a kid elephant is trained and on becoming an adult, such big elephant is just controlled by Mahawat and too with a small stick.

Still for knowledge of those who don't know, initially little elephant is tied with thick iron chain, and it's not able to move much. After some time the elephant realizes that, movement is not in its fate. This becomes its belief.

Even after becoming such big, elephant still moves under the instruction of the Mahawat.

Similarly, are your belief set by you or brands? I suggest you to take a break of two days and think what are the possibilities in your business.

Come out of the beliefs created by brands like:

1. This particular region is your territory

2. These are the products you can deal in

3. These are terms and conditions you need to follow to do business

Challenge your beliefs, and check for opportunities periodically. Keep networking with new people. Keep visiting new places. This will help you grow not only mentally, but spiritually as well.

CHAPTER-12

ENTRY AND EXIT IN THE DISTRIBUTION BUSINESS

Every distributor needs to understand that any product which is first launched and then it becomes a renowned brand, it goes through a journey. And let's try to understand this journey from a distributor's perspective.

1. The product is first launched and you become the initial distributor. At this point the risks are a bit high. But if you have avoided the mistakes mentioned in earlier chapters, the risk would be low.

2. Even though at this stage the risk is high, so is the return. Because, for the company you are the most important contact in the region given to you.

3. Slowly, the brand starts advertising and expanding its channel.

4. And there comes a stage when the product becomes a brand and it becomes a commodity (this I' m talking only about a product business).

5. Here, the profit margins are minimum and the company is at a stage wherein people are behind the executives to get the distribution.

6. This is the time for the distributor to decide, either to remain with the company and diversify because his efforts are minimum, or leave this company and repeat from stage 1, and find again a new product to start distribution.

Nothing I have understood in a single day. I have spent 15 years as a distributor and now owning a brand. In this journey, I have tried to understand the pains of the distributors. And hence, I am sharing with you all my experience.

CHAPTER-13

HOW TO APPLY LEARNING FROM THIS BOOK?

So my dear friends, please understand and apply the learning from this book.

Ramdas puthran from Udupi, **Vijeth kumar** from mysore, **Sathish g** from Mangalore have already subscribed to 10 million Rs. club... and are receiving support and our core expertise to grow their business. Within 2 years they are already doing approx 1 cr. Rs. of business.

I' m telling you guys, India is growing at a good pace. Our country is huge and has a big scope of business. **One**

stood business serves 100s. It's my deep concern that you take steps towards your success.

No one in this world is concerned neither to your growth nor to your money… I have seen several businesses. They start and close within 2 years.

We should not feel hesitant in taking help from people around.

If you feel that I can be of any help. You can book a 30 min. growth call with me or attend one of my webinars which I do regularly.

CONCLUSION

Phew !! So, finally we have come to the conclusion of this book. I feel a great sense of gratitude towards you for you have taken time to read this book.

Here are some recap of points:

1. Choose any brand for distribution with utmost care and choose brands which at least contribute to your growth

2. Focus on profits and not only on sales

3. It's your responsibility to grow your business, because it's you who have invested in it. It's you on whom your team looks up to

4. Be aware of upcoming challenges of business

5. Do not hesitate to ask help from experts, mentors

Do not forget to attend my webinar "double your profits in distribution business" and keep a watch on our new brand being launched with **Jasprit Bumrah** as our brand ambassador.

You can book a call with us to get help for your business. May be a 30 min. call with Sachin Agarwal, it can change the fate of your business.

Drop a mail to us on sachin@redonindia.com to get a chance to become a distributor of REDON brand in your city. Selling 30-40 crores rupees of material may not be important to earn wealth. In REDON, achieving reasonable targets may help you to create wealth for you and your family, with secured future in spite of the fact that ecommerce is booming, in spite of economy not doing too good.

For further learnings, lets connect on linkedin. My profile link is http://www.linkedin.com/in/ceosachinagarwal